A Life Beyond Limits
Overcoming Private Pain

Nataki Suggs

XY
Publishing

Published by
Xpress Yourself Publishing, LLC
P. O. Box 1615
Upper Marlboro, Maryland 20773

A Life Beyond Limits: Overcoming Private Pain
Copyright 2007 by Nataki Suggs

All Xpress Yourself Publishing, LLC's titles are available at special quantity discounts for bulk purchases for sales, promotions, premiums, fund-raising, educational or institutional use.

Special book excerpts or customized printings can also be created to fit specific needs. For details, write to Xpress Yourself Publishing, LLC, P.O. Box 1615, Upper Marlboro, MD 20773, Attn: Special Sales Department.

ISBN-10: 0-9792500-9-9
ISBN-13: 978-0-9792500-9-5

Cover Photography by

Cover and Interior Designed by The Writer's Assistant
www.thewritersassistant.com

*In loving memory of two of the strongest women I knew,
Naomi Ferebee-Battle and Alma Godwin, who greatly
influenced me through their tests, trials, and triumps.*

*And last, but not least, to my grandmother Leola Blackwell.
I may have never told you that you are one of the bravest
women I know. A widow left to raise eight boys and two
girls alone, Grandma, you will never be forgotten.*

*I am the Door: anyone who enters in through me will
be saved (will live). He will come in and he will go out
[freely], and will find pasture. The thief comes only in order
to steal and kill and destroy. I came that they may have
and enjoy life and have it in abundance (to the full, till it
overflows).
—John 10:9-10*

Dedication

This book is a tribute to every teenager who feels that they are forgotten, misunderstood, or a mistake. God loves you so much that He placed it on my heart to let you know what concerns you, concerns Him. You are the future leaders. I count it a privilege to be instrumental in planting a seed of hope through the gift of writing.

My prayer for you is that you will not accept society's opinion of you and that you will develop a true relationship with God. I remember when I was a teenager; I wished I could have had someone to invest in my spirituality so that at a young age, I could have realized that <u>with God all things are possible, if you believe!</u>

You deal with so much more than the generations before you. Allowing God to change your perception of what life means is key to fulfilling your true destiny on earth. We all want to experience being loved by someone. Why not receive the love through accepting the Lord Jesus Christ into your heart and I have to be honest…living a life following the blueprints that Christ left will not mean you won't have hardships. The blessing is that you have help to cope until the change comes and it will come.

Peace & Love,

Nataki

Acknowledgements

I would like to give thanks to Jesus Christ, the One who saved me from myself. I thank Him for this privilege to write and share with such transparency to others. Tre's, I love you, baby! You will always remain in my heart forever. Ma, thanks for being there for me through thick and thin. I love you, Ma! Uncle Rob, I love you for always being there for me when I was down. To my handsome kings, my sons, Destin and Josiah, Mommy loves you. You are the gifts that I will treasure forever. Chester, thanks for supporting me and being my friend through the good and the bad. To my dad, I love you. Aundrea Nelson, my Lord! Good looking out, sista'. You have truly been an angel sent by God to bring this book into existence. To my Aunt Markita, the last shall be first, remember that you are a diamond in the rough. Arkeatha Hawkins thanks for getting the ball rolling for this project. Thanks, baby! Thanks, Faye, for never judging me and for being a real friend. I would like to thank Drs. Randolph and Roxanna Perry, my pastors. Thank you for your continued spiritual counsel and prayers. To Evangelist Bernice Parker, thank you for praying me through this project.

To everyone who has been instrumental in encouraging me through words of prayer and listening ear—thank you.

And, finally, thanks again, God, for pushing me to a place where the opinions of men do not define who I am and to a place where I can tell the difference between the lies and the truth!

Table of Contents

Embrace all of the pain of your past because those things will give you color to the threads of the blanket of who you will become.

Life has no epidurals. Just as a woman is carrying a baby, the pain that life sometimes gives us is an indication of the birth that is soon to come.

Preface

Reading *A Life Beyond Limits: Overcoming Private Pain* by Nataki Suggs birthed from the joys and pains of life will convince you that she is a woman who is developing an intimate relationship with God. Nataki, in the writing of this work, gives credence to the thought that God often inspires us to produce a written chronology that reveals how He is able to sustain you with His peace, rest, and love. Some of the greatest works of the Bible were penned during seasons of great tribulation for the writer.

We know that you will feel both the pain of life and the goodness of God as you read *A Life Beyond Limits: Overcoming Private Pain*. Nataki Suggs has certainly been able to explore the deep riches of God's grace and mercy through her writings. If you think that this is just another collection of poems and stories, we encourage you to try a few riveting pages. You won't want to miss a word!

—*Dr. Randolph O. Perry, Senior Pastor of The Shepherd's House of Restoration*
—*Dr. Roxanna Perry, Pastor of The Shepherd's House of Restoration*

Introduction

In a perfect world, there are year-round beautiful skies, perfect weather, and peaceful intonations of every living thing; but the reality is, as these things work together, they do not always form a perfect balance. If you think about it, you will notice that there is a need for storms and disagreement because without them, one does not find truth or the strength that lies within. Many moods are displayed in the pages found in *A Life Beyond Limits: Overcoming Private Pain*. The expressions presented tell a story of my fears, passions, resolutions, and determination to rid my soul of all the agony and excitement of the trials and tribulations people go through.

I have a story to tell—some of it bad, but all of it true. As a young mother telling my story, you must remember that this is the story of how I came out of hiding, confronted the truth, and found freedom.

A Life Beyond Limits: *Overcoming Private Pain* depicts my struggle of confronting the truth about my past, illustrating how I was able to find stability and hope after I truly found God. My relationship with God created a stable foundation for me to continue climbing the ladder of success, confirming there is nothing I can do without Christ. Even when I could not see a glimmer of light at the end of the tunnel, I found that at the end, there was God's promise of freedom. As you read *A Life Beyond Limits: Overcoming Private Pain*, line by line, allow your heart to experience all of the hope that can be captured even when there seems to be none.

Betrayal from a Man

The title of this poem is self-explanatory…I was betrayed by a man.

The problem is that although it can be said with ease, it becomes difficult when you relive and deal with the pain of betrayal. When I was betrayed, there was no one around to console or push me to keep on living so I wrote this poem as encouragement to myself because this is what I felt someone should have said to me.

My betrayal stemmed from being hurt by someone I loved. I was cheated on, and this betrayal birthed distrust and more lies. Prior to the betrayal, I was at a place where I thought this person would never do that to me. Thus, when it happened, the actual sound of my heart breaking was unbearable. I was devastated to the point where I became depressed and began to doubt my self-worth.

For a period, I battled with depression. My self-esteem was challenged and, as time went on, it crumbled into nothingness. I felt as though I could never trust again. I began to ask the "what, when, why and how" questions because I was in such disbelief:

What is wrong with me?

When will this pain stop?

Why did this have to happen to me?

How could he do this to me?

These questions yielded themselves to feelings of determination. I was determined I would never be the one on the receiving end of betrayal's pain, so in some ways I became the betrayer. This was a vicious cycle until I actually dealt with the pain of being betrayed. Being the betrayer deceitfully made the pain subside because the relief was only temporary. It was not until I began to lean on God and His Word that I actually was able to feel real relief.

The question of why this could happen to me was answered when I looked at the life of Jesus. He said that I could not be exempt from persecution and pain because He was not. Keeping my faith in Him gave me relief because He loved, and continues to love, me pass the betrayal. He also shows me how to love others past the betrayal and, although it can be difficult, loving past betrayal yields to true forgiveness, which ultimately frees your mind, spirit, and heart.

Betrayal of a Man

Your Word says the servant is not greater than the master
So I bare the pain of being betrayed by a man...
A man who I planned to live happily ever after again,
But like a snake
He bit me with his venomous bait
I wish I can escape
The deep pain of the being betrayed by a man
A man, the one who I vowed to love, honor, and cherish,
The one who I married...
I believed he was the one;
Even so, I carried both of his sons

I never felt such heartbreak;
It hurts so bad...
I never imagined it would come from my mate...
You said in Your Word, you would not put more on me that I
can bear,
But the pain of betrayal seems to never end
You say You sticketh closer than a friend
So I say to You today LOVE me...my friend
The One who will never betray
The One who will be there till the end

He Said He Wouldn't Do it Again

As a child, I witnessed domestic violence. That vicious cycle repeated itself through several relationships and me. I often wondered why I would continue to allow myself to connect with men who had problems with uncontrollable anger. I, too, struggled with fits of rage and often lashed out on family members and associates. The seed of that learned behavior began to grow over the years, which resulted in me attracting men who were controlling and overly aggressive. I thought love from a man meant he had to display an aggressive, thuggish swagger. It took me to experience much heartache to realize that I deserved to be loved in a way that did not mean being belittled or physically attacked.

I had to experience abuse in a relationship, in which I thought it would never happen, for me to wake up. I had to reevaluate myself and think about what was in me that I would allow myself to be treated like that. I had to separate myself from this particular person so I could begin to soul search and revisit past issues in my life. I had to begin to love myself to realize that abuse is not something you should accept from anyone. Loving me was the first step to understanding I was worth being loved the way God intended me to be.

Being in an abusive relationship, especially with someone you love, can be devastating, and crippling to your progress in moving forward in life. No man or woman deserves to be verbally or physically attacked by anyone. The fear that grips you is something that can be conquered through first accepting that abuse is not a part of God's purpose and plan for your life. We were created to coexist in relationships with harmony, understanding and, most of all, with love. I hope my journey to recovery can encourage those who have been victims to the tragedy of this serious issue that many families face. Moreover, my hope is that you know you are not alone and you can be victorious in the end.

You pretend that you're okay
So you stay in the place
Where you feel you can't escape
But I'm here to say, "You're not alone!"
So please pick up the phone
And reach out for help from someone else
Who understands the abuse you're taking from that man
Don't believe the lie that you are by yourself
Because of your lack of help from someone else...

Just don't give up, you have been through enough
God loves you and He has a greater purpose in
store for you
He sees your shame and feels your pain that you contain
The black eyes, the fights at night,
The constant thoughts of even taking your life...
The hidden bruises, the verbal abuse
And knowing that others who know you
Don't even have a clue of what you're really going
through...

The living in hell that you can't tell
Most of the time it overwhelms you
To the point you say to yourself:
"What's going on? Why me?

I just want to be free
To live at peace and not in all of this insanity"

God is watching, He feels your pain, and sees your shame
He will turn it around and make you whole one day...
God loves you, He will cover you
He will protect you from all that oppresses you...
Don't be deceived, you can be free!
Just step out on faith and I guarantee, you will escape...

He said he won't do it again,
He has problems and you can't solve them...
So get the help and most of all take care of yourself
Your purpose, you will never know
Unless you take a chance and let it go...
Just step aside and let God be your guide
Yea, though you walk through the valley of the
shadow of death
Remember fear no evil, because God will never leave you.

The Fight to Stay

I am not sure about you, but I have never experienced a manifested rest. I am always in an inward battle. In the Bible, Apostle Paul said it best when he said, "The good that I would do, evil is always present," because it is always a struggle between good and evil. It is hard to express this to people because sometimes people blow you off with comments like, "Oh it's not all that," "You alright," but this is not the truth. While I may feel alone in this, I know I am not out here by myself. I truly desire to do the right thing. I guess that is why it is such a struggle. I want to stay grounded in the Word and I know it is a fight. Even when I do bad things, I desire to do well.

In everything that I do, I realize there is always a fight with flesh. Even going through the battle, desiring these things, you realize you have so many enemies, not only inwardly but outwardly. It really gets rough when the struggle becomes exposed. People that may seem to be there for you may not really have good intentions. These same people are sometimes there just waiting for you to fall. They are not there to help or lend a helping hand, to understand where you are, be an ear to listen to you or be there to realize that they too have struggles.

However, they are judging you and looking at you without even considering the struggles they are going through.

For those of you who are struggling, or have struggled with the strongholds of lust, envy, jealousy, bitterness, uncontrollable anger, greed, maliciousness, self-hatred, adultery, drug addiction, arrogance, selfish-pride, and depression, this poem, *The Fight to Stay,* is for you. Some of these things I have dealt with, and still have to fight to overcome them, but I know that I have to keep fighting to stay on this path. I fight to stay because I want to be a true believer and a true reflection of what I profess. I fight to stay because I want to be free from the flesh and free from the things that try to rule me. I fight to stay because I need the peace. I fight hard to stay because sin, although pleasurable at times, is never good for you. It may feel good at the moment, but the consequences of what you do will shield to much heartache, and the heartache may not even be yours.

Backsliding...I can't deny
I've done it several times
Even though I did,
The One who loves me
Continued to call me back to the place
Where I would be safe
From the bad choices I had made
Which delayed my journey towards my destiny.

I've traveled down so many wrong places
That caused me to be in a frustrated state
My mind was double...
A part of me wanted to be free from the struggle
The good I wanted to do
But evil was always present
And it seemed as though
My flesh would not let go
So I could grow
To be in a place where righteousness has its way
Not good to the point where I appear better than anyone,
Just right in the sight of the Almighty,
The One who sent His Son
The One who defeated the evil one

Fight to Stay

In the midst of it all…
He was the One who never stopped loving me
Because I was wrong
The lies that my mind would tell me,
"It can't be done,"
"I'm only human,"
I began to see the connection
That without His direction
I wouldn't be able to fight this flesh
So I embrace the faith everyday
So I can be content within
Because now I know He holds the power
To give you strength to conquer many sins
Day to day I look to Him to get the strength
So I can continue to win
Each battle that the devil sends

A work in progress
Each minute, each second
I'm to the point, I'm just glad to be on the right road to
freedom
Free to be honest about me,
You see, blame brings shame
And will drive you close to being insane.

So I make the choice to be honest with myself
So I can receive the help.

Now I know that it is God that has the true power
In my weakest hour
To help me to escape the fight within
So that I can conquer my many sins
If it means being different because I choose righteousness
And not following the world's system,
I'd rather please the One who gives me the conviction
To do the right thing
In spite of what life's trials and tribulations may bring.

Taking the Mask Off

I titled this poem, *Taking the Mask Off* because I was not true to myself. I was living a lie, believing I was well mentally and spiritually. I did not have peace of mind and spirit. I ran from the pain I deeply felt. I was like a fugitive running from my own life. I did not want to face the fact that I had to confront the many issues I hid for so many years. It was too real, it was too painful, and it was too true.

The truth is something we should embrace; but when truth taps you on the shoulder, we ignore it. Why do we ignore the truth? What is it about the truth that we do not want to confront? Is it too painful? Is it like staring in the mirror? My truth was that I was very bitter and angry about so many things and at so many people who had hurt me. I covered up the pain by getting into many unhealthy relationships. My choice of what I thought were good friendships always ended. Either we stopped speaking or it would be something very stupid that would cause resentment between both parties. It got to the point where I only embraced a few people to be within my circle.

When I turned thirty-one, something very devastating happened to me. My youngest son was diagnosed with Autism. I began to feel many strange emotions. The news of his diagnosis triggered the pain I had been carrying for thirty-one years! It took me seeing my child struggle, with so many challenges, that I had to come clean so I could be there for him and my oldest son. If I did not deal with my own issues, I could not effectively help him with his. The saying "God works in mysterious ways" is true, because having a child with special needs became training for me to birth out love, forgiveness, compassion, and patience. It pushed me to answer the tap of truth that was standing next to me the whole time.

I had to be honest with myself so God could heal me because self-denial is like playing Russian roulette. One day you may fire a round, if you keep pulling the trigger. I realize how life is a journey and in order to survive life's trials and tribulations, you need a tour guide to warn you of the one-ways, the detours, the cliffs, and dead ends. My tour guide is the Lord. Although my grandmother took me to church, I did not believe in God because I was a victim of pain and I blamed Him. When I turned twenty-four, I began to believe because, by that time, I had so many life and death moments that I had to believe that a higher power was in operation for me.

In 2005, I was struck with viral meningitis to the membrane. I was hospitalized for two weeks. My kidneys began to shut down and if it were not for God answering the prayers of people and my own faith in Him, I know I would not be here now. Now at thirty-three, I am taking God and life seriously. I cannot be phony with others or myself. For what? God is my judge and

He knows me better than I know myself. I truly believe He was with me all along. Facing the truth about you can cause you not to sweat the small stuff and to accept people for who they are, without being judgmental. We all have things we struggle with, whether it is privately or openly, but we must take off the mask so we can uncover those hidden things that can only harm us if we do not have truth.

When swelling [being puffed up, having the "big-head"] and pride comes, then emptiness and shame come also, but when the humble (those who are lowly, who have been pruned [stripped] or chiseled by trial, renounce self [self-guidance]) are skillful [then comes] Godly-wisdom and soundness (Proverbs 11:2 AMP).

Wearing a mask is a part of my past.
I felt low inside...
In spite of how many times
I was told I was easy on the eyes.
I wore a mask on my face
To cover the pain that I faced everyday.
Makeup and other stuff I used to cover up
The realness of who I was and how I felt about myself.
As years go by, I've begin to realize
Who I thought I was, was a lie.
And there is much more to me than the outside.
I was defining myself according to the pain.
It has opened my eyes to see how people live a lie.
Many people, too, have tremendous pain inside.

I've been told that the eyes are the windows to the soul.
So many look good on the outside
And have private pain that they can't explain,
Because of the shame.
So we pretend that we are OK
And wear a phony face from day to day.
Be real and I guarantee, you will be healed
From the years of pretending that you're whole
in your soul.

So let it go and give it to the One
Who can give you peace in your time of need.
You see I'm talking to the one who thinks that they got
it going on.
Success can't give you that true rest that conquers
life's test.
Peace is the thing that we need to live this life abundantly.

Young Girl

This poem is dedicated to young girls.

Times have surely changed. Image is so commercialized in the media and it corrupts the minds of so many young girls. It seems as though the way you look defines who you are in today's society. We have so many young girls who are struggling with eating disorders, low self-esteem and self-hatred because they feel they do not meet the standard of what society views as beautiful. For years, I struggled with my weight and, honestly, my whole image. I began to realize that it was very important to love the skin you are in. This came from years of believing I truly was not beautiful, regardless of what people thought.

Working with young people in the school system awakened a need to be a positive voice in poetry to impart some truth to young girls. Being thin, having long hair, or wearing the latest fad does not define you as a person. The outer should only enhance the inner beauty. When I look into the eyes of the students I meet, or a young girl in the mall or grocery store, I see how I used to be. Beyond the outer, I see pain and wanting to be accepted to fit the "standard of beauty." We were all created in His image and after His likeness (Genesis 1:26).

Now, beauty, to me, means to embrace the fact that God did not make a mistake when He formed me in my mother's womb. Beauty is to be picked by the Almighty to enter into time and fulfill the purpose that He ordained for me to accomplish. Beauty is knowing that I am so loved by God; He designed me as authentic and not a copy. Beauty is the mere blessing to be at a place in my life to awaken the beauty in people who have no clue of how special they are to the One who created them. Beauty, you see, is a truth that only comes when you can become confident in the fact that it is more than outer appearance; beauty is in the love that God has for you.

Young girl, do not define yourself according to the
world's system,
Which tells you, "If you don't look like a star, you
won't go far."
You are beautiful inside
And not by what man may see on the outside.
Your size, you may despise
Because of the image that society recognizes.
Don't be fooled! These videos you watch are just not true.
I plead with you young girl, God loves you.

Do you have a clue of how precious you are to the One
who created you?
He will show you your worth
And not what's under your skirt.
He longs to be your closest friend
And, not the kind who will just pretend.
You are a diamond in the ruff,
But when you see yourself, you don't feel good enough.
You're created in the image of the Almighty,
The One who gave you your life to live,
Be encouraged, you are worth it.
Young girl, you are blessed

Young Girl

And He will guide you through all of life's tests.
No matter how many times you fall,
God is love and He loves you most of all!

Damaged Goods

It started very early in my childhood. My grandmother, who is no longer living life here anymore, is now resting in eternity with the Creator. She would tell me never leave the house without lipstick on or without the best attire. "You don't know who you may see," she would say to me. Those words were embedded in my mind.

I have always had a good eye for fashion and cosmetics and, most of all, hair. My looks became a means of self-worth. If I did not look up to the standard of what people thought, I did not feel good about myself. Being a teenager was the beginning of the monster being birthed. I desired to be best dressed and most desired by the opposite sex, which I thought defined who I was. As I began to desire a relationship with the Lord, a light switch came on. I had begun to see myself in other women and I did not like what I saw. I felt superficial most of the time, especially the older I got. What was manifested on the outside was not how I felt within.

I desired to be beautiful, not only outside but inside, as well. I felt like a caterpillar in a cocoon, waiting to break free from the place where I was being held back from spreading my wings of beautiful colors. It was when I began to read and learn what God's Word says about me and how He makes everything beautiful in His time, that I started to understand what it means to be beautiful. God gave me beauty for ashes.

I wore a garment of heaviness and depression. I wanted to please people and was always concerned about their opinions of me. Now my worth is in the love that God has for me. My reputation is now in how God sees me. I live to please Him through sharing the blessing of living beyond the pain of my past. It is a reminder of how, through it all, I am still here and have a chance to tell others how they can become whole through the love of God.

The Prada
The Marc Jacobs
The Mac makeup
The weave in your hair
So you get the stares
The short mini skirts
So the men will go berserk

But when you're alone
You feel an empty void
You shop to ignore what's really going on
It's nothing wrong with looking good
Just make sure you deal with the real you
Material things cannot take away the pain
It's like a junkie who needs a quick fix

We cover up with the latest stuff
But inside, you're crying for help
The baggage that we carry like low self esteem
You know what I mean
You look in the mirror
And you think that you're superior

The silent pain…
You can't explain
So you play the game that most hurting women play
When you are alone the reality of who you are
Apart from the outer stuff
You really don't feel good enough
You camouflage with weight loss, fancy cars
And, the image of looking like a star

The truth of the matter is…
The pain, you can't handle
So believe in the One who can break the emotional chains
That hold you captive
So you can be free to see
That you are more than the outer beauty
You are the apple of His eye
Who?
The Creator, the One who really loves you

The Controlling Woman

I wrote this poem because I can identify with wanting to have control over everything and everybody that was in my life. Being in control stemmed from feelings of insecurity and feeling rejected throughout my childhood. I did not realize I was a controlling person until I saw relationships end because I became co-dependent on the need to rule, especially with men. I do believe that everyone has a choice to make. We are all responsible for our decisions, but when it crosses over into manipulation and domination, it is wrong. We should never try to control another person's will, subliminally. For example, some women use their body to control men and vice versa. Some people use money and their influence to control others. More examples are: a wife who withholds intimacy from her husband as a means of punishment because of something simple he did not do; a man who abuses his wife or children to get them to listen; and the abuse of leadership (this includes churches that control people to the point where they follow man instead of God). I have learned that a true leader understands that in order to lead, you may have to give up control and follow first.

The Controlling Woman

Control,
She's in a role that she's playing
To feel needed by people who are near,
Which she tries to hold dear.
Her self-esteem must be low
So she tries to blow her own self up.
She seems to be puffed up
In pride...that leads to a fall and then she won't stand tall.

The role of control can get old to those who know her
ways.
Sometimes they won't say anything because they are afraid
So they pretend to comprehend,
But it's not cool to overrule... all the time.
Everyone can feel that control vibe most of the time.
The need to be needed is a human feeling,
But she abuses it by wanting to feel supreme.
You know what I mean...
By always trying to be seen
Or being head of the team.

Chill out!
You won't lose clout... if you can settle down.
And people will come around
To see that you are worth havin' on the team.

Brokenness

I had to get broken down to understand that God is the One that needs to have complete control over my life. My brokenness happened through hardship, that is why in the poem I say, "Being broken is no joke" because you do not become broken by mere words. You become broken through many difficulties, trials, and tests. As some people go through these hardships, either they become further separated from God or they become more dependent on God and begin to draw closer to Him. Those who draw closer to Him, begin to realize that He is. They realize that He is the mender of every mistake, heartache, and bad choice. They get the understanding that He is the One who can ultimately bring some clarity to everything they went through in their lives, whether good or bad.

The brokenness that inspired me to write this poem had me to a point where all I could say was, "Yes, God! I believe that You are there. I believe that You are who You say You are. I believe that You have the power to make me whole as a person. You have the power to change my mindset so that I won't define myself according to my past experiences." This same brokenness caused me to become humble in my entire being. It was definitely a journey. It is still my daily journey to become humble before

God and know that I am not here because of my own strength. He is there and He is the One that knows me better than I know myself.

Being broken is no joke

Being broken brings humility
Which is the only road to deliverance
From this flesh which is a total mess…
Being broken takes you to a place
Where you can't escape
The potter's hand
That will put the pieces back together again.

Brokenness drove a woman to touch the hem of the
Savior's garment

Don't misunderstand
I'm not talking about the money that's not in your hand…
I'm speaking of being broken before the Father,
The One that you should follow
He's the potter and we are the clay,
He desires to put us back together
Day by day, He will take you to a place
Where you can escape the mistakes that we make
everyday…

Brokenness produces a new you,

A person who longs to love the Lord
As much as He loves you
A vessel, a servant,
Oh yes being used by the Master of our souls
The only One who can make you whole
And fill every void you have not told

Brokenness will cause you to depend on the One
Who sent His only begotten son...

The True Believer

I am writing this because of experiences I went through in going to what we call "church."

I say this because some things that people associate with church or with being a Christian are not true. Being a Christian does not mean being without sin. It means that you are at a place where you are allowing God to develop your character. You are following the life of Jesus and striving to be a representative and a model of what He stood for, which involves loving everybody. Not just loving people that are the closest to you, but loving everybody from the drug addict to the poor person, the prostitute to the robber, the troubled teen to the businessman, the preacher to the teacher, the convict to the bus driver, the housewife to the celebrity.

Being introduced to church, I saw the opposite of what Jesus stood for. He came for the broken hearted. He came for the down trodden, the drug addict, the prostitute, the gambler. He did not just come for those who profess Him. Being a true believer means that you are actively striving to be a real reflection of God and strive to exude his characteristics of caring, loving, and sharing. It goes beyond going to a building, knowing many Scriptures, and having many members. It's about healing the broken hearted, giving hope to the hopeless, perfecting our character, integrity, serenity, and being different from how man views being "good."

I was inspired to write this because, in my experience, I saw more of the opposite of what Jesus stood for. Now I understand why Jesus said not to just clean the cup on the outside but to also clean the inside too (Matthew 23:25-27). Writing this was the beginning process of me being cleansed from the inside out because the message is always to the messenger first. I also wrote this to encourage people who have been hurt by the misrepresentation of people who have professed to follow Christ to know what it really means to be a believer.

Judging people seems to be the thing
That many who believe in the Lord do daily
Who are we to throw stones at the ones who God, one day
may call home?

Man looks at the outer
But God looks at the heart from the very start
Some wear their long skirts and their Jesus T-Shirts
And will step over the one in need
Most of the time it's the drunk on the street
But they say they believe...
Believe in who?

As I recall Jesus loved even the thief and the murderer on
the cross too
Sin has no category
If you are sleeping with a different man
Or even smoking or doing dope
Or lying and even having bitterness, pride, and selfishness
inside
Or even hating another person within
Judge not, lest you will be judged
God has the final say so and we don't
Jesus came not to condemn the world,

But through Him, they would be saved from the penalty of sin
That let's me know that judging people is not a true
representation of following Jesus

It's not about all of the Scriptures you know…
It's about the love that you are supposed to show
People are struggling with tremendous pain
So watch how you approach people in His name

Jesus was moved with compassion
He understood that man needed a helping hand
He never came to condemn
His purpose was to show God's love to all men

If we as Christians can one day realize
We're not to turn up our nose at anybody
*When you become free, from those things that had **you** in*
the same place
Remember to never judge another person's weakness in
anyway
Walk in humility!
And on that day when all are judged
He will say, "I'm pleased because I saw a reflection of
Me!"

The Dreamer

I have always felt that greatness was my portion…my piece of the pie. Even though I went through having a not-so-stable childhood, and dealing with confusion and lack of self-love, I always dared to dream big. I can remember, as a young child, longing to be a leader and a person of influence. I remember wanting to be happy…if nothing else just to be a happy person to overcome the pain of rejection and the feeling of being an outcast within. I can remember sitting and looking at the sky, dreaming of being ahead and being able to say, "I made it!"

I did not understand why I stayed in a consistent state of imagining. Even when I went to bed at night, I would wake up from a dream that indicated that where I was in my life was not where I would always be. I can recall telling others about my dreams and the responses would vary. Some would laugh and some would simply ignore what I was saying. But, I could not stop dreaming! I mean, you live to dream, a sure promise that you are destined for something greater than where you are.

The Dreamer

You begin to feel the need to believe
Because of the dreams you conceive.
You can't even see
But you dream to be the reality of your most inner thoughts
That project in the most profound ways.
It's like a movie premiere
Of what is to come near.
It continues to encourage you to pursue the mental clues
Of what is in store for you.
Sometimes it seems so hard to reach,
Because of the magnitude of the dream.
It's a prophetic reminder of the possibilities
That God has in store for those who believe.
Dream Big!
And you will achieve
What you have seen while asleep
Or even in a day dream.

Be Honest

I wrote this poem because I was physically tired of people lying to me and being fake. I questioned who really was real in my life and wondered if people could really be honest.

Generally, in the beginning of a relationship, it is very difficult to know if the person you allow into your life is there for a reason, a season, or a lifetime. Most of my life, unfortunately, I have had many encounters with individuals who were wolves in sheep's clothing. I was very naive when it came to picking the right acquaintances, and so called friends.

Inside, I always felt a premonition that they were not for me, but because of my own need of wanting to be accepted, I continued with those relationships until it was exposed that they were counterfeits. As the years have gone by, I began to look at the life of Jesus and realize He endured much more pain and hurt in relationships, mainly from the people closest to him. The betrayal by Judas propelled him to fulfill his divine purpose on earth, and that was to die for all humanity.

If my Jesus could continue to press forward, even though he was despised, rejected, misunderstood, and betrayed, why can't I? He is my example. His suffering was instrumental in

Him obtaining the power that He now holds. This example helped me to understand that your enemies can really become a tool that God allows into your life to spark the fire and the passion to pursue harder towards your divine purpose and destiny.

I'm tired of people being fake with me
They act as though I don't see
They say with their mouth
They are truly down for me
But inwardly
They wait for me to fall
So they can stand tall
I'm holding on, even though I'm going through the storm
I don't know how long 'til my change comes
But I keep pressing on

I've had so many ups and downs, setbacks,
disappointments,
And even sometimes feeling hopeless
I realize that the real prize...is believing
In spite of how many fights this life may bring
Which can cause some people to be close to being insane
Because of the pain
That hardship brings

Every situation I will win in the end
Because of He who lives in me,
You see Christ died for all creation to see that
He defeated the things that life can bring:
Betrayal, rejection, being misunderstood,

Be Honest

Accused falsely for something He didn't even do...
What kind of man can endure so much pain
And arise with all power in His hand?
He is my hope that if I believe
Then I, too, can conquer all that life throws at me.

43

You Shall Live and Not Die

I always felt like a dark cloud hovered over me. It started when I was five years old because I was molested from age five to eight years old. I remember feeling empty and not knowing why until I had begun to live a destructive life. Unfortunately, during this destructive life, I was raped. I had the uncontrollable need to self-destruct because of the pain of the act and the pain of my dad not being there to protect and really father me. I was searching and longing for that space, that void to be filled. I started to live a riotous life because *I* did not love me.

I had never experienced unconditional love. This led to me being almost like the walking dead, being dead to my emotions, and how I really felt. Until I had a real encounter with God, I did not realize that the root of my pain or my walking death was my molestation. It was damaging to my life and me. It was as if I was living, yet dying inside, pretending that everything was okay but inwardly not even wanting to exist.

It was not until I confronted the truth that I could accept the fact that life was really worth living. We are all created in the image of God and we all have a purpose. I believe that we are all made with a space inside of us that only God can fill. It took years of bad relationships, wanting to fit in, and professional help to realize it was not my fault and I was a victim, an unwilling participant and a pawn to aid in the self-gratification of another. After realizing this, the healing process was able to start because I was able to see what this emptiness was.

What inspired me to write *A Life Beyond Limits: Overcoming Private Pain* was my wanting to encourage everyone that has had something to cripple, devastate, or alter his or her life. I wanted to remind people that pain is not a respecter of persons. It is something that we all experience. No one is exempt. Pain will always find its way into your life, whether it be something as small as a paper cut or as big as a migraine headache. My story is meant to aid in the initiation of your healing because I am a survivor of pain and I know that pain can be eliminated, once you know its root. Pain's weakness is knowledge. Once you know and recognize pain, you can begin to counteract its effects with hope, healing, or the longing to be healed. Once your emotions begin to line up with living, then pain has no choice but to wither away. This is why it is necessary to believe, say, and know that you can and shall live and not die.

For God hath not given us the spirit of fear; but of power, and of love, and of a sound mind (II Timothy 1:7 KJV).

You may feel low inside
Because of sex, money and lies
I say to you, you shall live and not die

Life has been very hard for you,
The struggle seems never ending
And most of the time you pretend you are winning

Your future is so bright,
Just be prepared to fight the good fight...
Of faith, we should embrace from day to day

The pain inside may be great
And you feel you can't escape this place
Of where you feel life is not worth living
Please don't believe that's the only way out of the maze,
Just continue to take it day by day...

It would be a shame if you don't get to see
What the creator destined for you to be,
All you need is to believe
In the One who can deliver you from all insanity...

The pain of your past or even the present wears you down,
Most of the time you ware a frown...

Know you are special and you are loved
Especially from the One above.

Love is something you may not know,
But I guarantee, He will never let you go...
Hold on, help is on the way,
I, too, felt the same pain and thought it would never end...

The Last Shall Be First

God promises that the last shall be first, but, as one continues to be looked over, this promise becomes harder to believe. It is almost as if you wear a sign on your forehead that says, "Don't pick me first!" You may even become wayward in your thinking and believe that you are not worth being first, which gives way to you settling for second-rate things. You may also begin to become envious or jealous of others because they always seem to get ahead while your situation never seems to change.

The feeling of being last caused me to dream. I dreamt of having things go my way for a change. I dreamt of being picked first. I even dreamt of being a writer. However, I did not really think that I could achieve any of those dreams, so procrastination and slothfulness became my running partners. Finally I realized that the dreams I had were not just mere dreams, they were indicators of my desire to be first, blessed, happy, whole, and content.

I wanted a real relationship with God. Stumbling upon a scripture that confirmed these desires caused me to write it down in poetry. I also wrote this poem to encourage others who have always felt that they were in second place, or in the shadow of a sibling, cousin, or even the last choice in a group of friends. I wanted each person to know that last is not always a bad place because it can be said that some 'save the best for last.'

"But many who [now] are first will be last [then], and many who [now] are last will be first [then]" (Matthew 19:30 AMP).

You may feel forgotten
You may even feel that it's too late to escape
From being in second place
But rest assure roles will reverse
And you will be first in line
Delayed but not denied
The chance to advance in this life
Because of the many fights
And the blows that never seem to go

But I will say one day...
This will go away
Just believe, know, have faith in God and the last will be
first
Stay strong; hold on,
The storms will pass you by
And then you will be blessed to see why you made it
through life's tests

God will straighten the crooked places that you have been
facing
Then you will receive your divine destiny...
These tests of your faith

Will keep you holding on day by day
He sees all, knows all,
And is the One who will open the door

I know it hurts...
But God promised in His Word that the last shall be first.

Real Love and Love

I was inspired to write these poems because I always yearned for love, but then I found myself always running into roadblocks and brick walls. But, through my journey of trying to live according to how Jesus would want us to live, I began to long for what God says love is and not what man says it is. In my longing, I realized that in most of my life, I never received real love and I never recognized the love that God has for us. I was never exposed to the truth of what love is until I sought after God and His word.

In *Real Love* it says, "Love cares and never fears" because I was filled with so much fear in my life of not being love, but I now know that love should not fear. Love also never fails and is faithful. This statement comes from being betrayed. I just believe that if you really love someone then you are loyal…not perfect…but loyal. "Love is strong" and nobody should be able to come in and break the bond of love that you have, not just for people, but the love that you have for God and His love for you (I Corinthians 13).

God is showing me truth everyday and everyday is a journey. What I thought love was is not what love really is. I believe that love is so much more than what the human mind can comprehend. It originates from God and He is bigger than we are. These poems were inspired by pain I was going through. God's love for me kept me each day. It was only His love and, when I say that it was His love, He just loved me through it. He kept me when I did not want to be kept.

Love that last never keeps a record of the past
Love should progress by passing every test
Love cares and should never fear
Love stands for the best and should never
believe anything less

Love never betrays, but is faithful everyday
Love is strong, so always hold on
Love never hates, so believe in the One
Who gives us life to live everyday.

Love conquers all even when we may fall
Love is not a feeling but a way of living
Love is power even in your weakest hours
Love supersedes pain
Even when you feel you can't make it day to day

Love is patient, love is kind
Love will believe the best and not any lies
God is love!
So set your affection on things above

To My Mom
With Love,

Taki

LOVE

*LOVE is **What?***

A relationship, a marriage, a friend?

A child, a mother, a father, a sister, or a brother?

Love says, "I'm long suffering, patient, and kind."

Love sees no fault

In a man's walk

Love believes the best

Even when we are in a test

It rests...

Like the dew in the morning

Resting upon your heart

You cannot be apart

From the very start

It is the rest

That LOVE gives in the midst of a test

Who is LOVE?

Is it a feeling?

An emotion?

No, it is the foundation of who He is inside

Where His Spirit resides...

Who resides?

The author the finisher of our faith, the Savior, the Master,

Our hope to cope

Real Love and Love

Who is LOVE?
LOVE is! LOVE was!
LOVE will be with you:
To comfort you
To protect you
To beckon you to come,
Come...
Love is calling
It standeth at the door
And it's knocking at your heart
From the very start
It will never leave you or forsake you, it will take you
higher
Higher as an eagle flies

LOVE is coming for you on that day
To take us away
To a better place
Seek it, be it, believe it, take it and embrace it
Let no one take the place of it

LOVE is what we need...

So be ready beloved
I'm coming for LOVE on that day,
And don't be surprised...
Because your redemption draws nigh!

God Is Not like Man

In a religion, you have to appease God in order to receive something from Him. When you serve Christ and walk in His ways, you automatically obtain eternal spiritual wealth. Religion is a manmade imitation of trying to be good enough to be accepted by God Almighty. It is the power of the Savior to reveal the truth of redemption through Him giving His life as a ransom for the penalty of man's fall in Eden by Adam. *For my thoughts are not your thoughts, neither are your ways my ways saith the Lord* (Isaiah 55:8).

God's love is everlasting; it is who He is and who He will always be. His desire is to establish a relationship with His creation. The greatest fulfillment in a man's soul is a reconnection to the One whom created him. God can take the years of pain you carry and begin to heal you and awaken your spirit man. It is an awareness of the love that you always desired to be restored in your heart. Knowing that God is in control and that His abiding presence is around you, illuminating through you, is all you need.

God is faithful, He is just
He is the only One I can really trust.
He guides me and protects me,
Rest assure, He will never close the door.
He standeth at the door and is knocking at the hearts of
man,
I realize that He wants to come in
And ease the pain and take away many sins.
His love for me is eternal,
Which means it has no end.

I've searched all my life to find a love,
Which is unconditional and pure.
I never imagined in my wildest dreams,
It would come from the Lord.
I've longed for this kind of love from all types of
relationships
Including my mother, my father and different relationships
with men.
His ways cannot be explained,
It's beyond human reasoning.
The mind can't even comprehend
I'm starting to realize that God is really not like man.

This moment as I express my deepest desires,
I pray that He will endow me with some of that same
power
To love, to trust, to really have unconditional love.
I dare to dream that I, too, can share with others
The kind of love you can't get from no other.
Not by might, not even by human power, but by God's
spirit,
I conquer by letting go of all hurt and painful feelings.
Life is worth it and I look forward to living it.
I end by really understanding that God is not like man.

God's Gift

I dedicate this poem to anyone who deals with or has dealt with a relative who has or had special needs. You are not alone. I know your pain. I know your struggle.

Having a child with special needs can be hard at
times to believe
God is the one who can fulfill their true destiny
It's hard at times to comprehend why society judges them
But I stand to see how the Creator who made all men
Can do great things with them…
And they can make it like all men

The stares and the whispers in the stores, malls and
even in some homes
*The special ones are God's creation and **yes** they*
are truly blessed
So I say to you it's only a test, a test of your faith
Hold on and you will begin to see why they are here
The purpose the Almighty destined for them to be…
They are fearfully and wonderfully made
So take it day by day and remember to keep the faith

Patience, love and kindness can be developed with a child
Who has certain challenges...
Begin to embrace what you continue to face
You will win in the end, especially if you show love to them

Freedom

You can become incarcerated in your mind and not know how to escape. For me, it was as if I had withered away into an outer darkness. My vision was blinded by experiences, which included mental abuse. I was shackled in my way of thinking and my perception of what life meant was tainted. It did not help that I fed the appetite of this state by believing the lies of those who did not realize that they were aiding and abetting the illegal warden of my mind. I made a decision, a simple decision to allow myself to open up to the possibilities of pursuing a life of believing that God could heal me and give me the keys to unlock the shackles that held me in bondage for so many years. It was revealed to me that I had help all along, but I did not know it. The keys to unlocking the shackles were next to me the whole time! All I had to do was pick up those keys and set myself free.

I cannot speak for anyone else, but this journey of freedom can be hard at times because when you have been bound for so long, you are not used to being free. It is like people who are released from the prison system after being incarcerated for so many years. When they are released, it is like shell shock because everything has changed and they have to adjust to the fact that life has moved on without them. Everyday, to me, is a day to celebrate that no matter what the reality is…I am out! I have been released! Everyday I make a conscious decision to choose freedom. This is an out-of-box mentality.

It is so liberating when you can accept the truth that what did not kill you can only be a blessing. Now I only accept what God says about me through His word. Why wouldn't I believe Him? He set me free! He holds the key to man's purpose and His desire is for man to love Him just as much as He loves us. I write this to give hope to those who feel like they are in captivity in their minds. Fear, depression, rejection, frustration, the pain of your past, inferiority, and emotional trauma are all shackles. God can and He will heal you. I am living proof that He can begin the process of healing in your life and, most of all, in your mind.

A butterfly flies free, but only the butterfly knows the process of how it became so beautiful—from a caterpillar to a striking, free-spirited creation.

I'm free to be me,
The one who is free to fulfill her destiny
I can see clearly
So I wipe my tears away
I say to my past,
"I knew it wasn't going to last!"
I feel better than ever
The joy inside, I cannot deny

I've tried to get help
Because of the way I felt about myself
The deep pain that I silently agonized in day after day
And day after day...
I just wanted it to go away
So each day I longed for freedom from the pit that I fell in
I could not get out because fear was near
And I was told it was
***F**alse **E**vidence **A**ppearing **R**eal*

Then one day I prayed for the day to stand toe- to- toe
To the truth of who I had become...
I tried to run from the One who could fill the hole
That was in my soul
I then decided it was me
And the pain that was so deep in me

Freedom

It was holding me captive
To the point I didn't know what was happening
Until I embraced the truth that being free was the key
To fulfilling all that God had for me to be...
So, I believe in the One who opens your eyes
To realize
That the pain that some people carry is too heavy to
contain
I confess it to the One who sent His only begotten son,
Who says you can live in joy and peace and can fulfill that
inner need.

Real life means being whole in your soul
You can be at peace
And not close to being insane
From feeling that tremendous pain, I called on His name
The name that is above every name
The Prince of Peace, the One who saved and transformed
me to be free
So I can tell others how they can recover.
That if thou shalt confess with thy mouth the Lord Jesus,
and shalt believe in thine heart that God hath raised him from
the dead, thou shalt be saved.

Encouraging Words to Live By

You can experience pain in a number of ways. If we were to address pain, we could say that pain is "the distress or suffering, mental or physical, caused by great anxiety, anguish, grief or disappointment." Pain can become an isolating ache, which drags you back and detaches you from a world that to most appears normal.

Understanding that you're not alone in your pain...all of humanity at some point has experienced a segment of pain. Pain enslaves people and is not so easy for some to release. My focal point is not so much on your pain, but it's on the fact that you can let go of pain. You can experience the freedom that was intended for you from the inception of this world. God loves you, and what touches you, touches Him, what affects you, affects Him. It is His desire for you to be whole. Letting go of the pain is not a task that can be accomplished alone. God wants to help you release, not some, but all of what entangles your being and prohibits you from moving forward. He wants to help you conquer this affliction so that you can move forward. He wants to be there for you...you are not alone.

As difficult as this may sound, you must first forgive those who hurt you, be it mentally or physically, and release them. Forgive and release, even if the person has passed on. In forgiving and releasing them, your freedom is at hand. You have purpose, you have destiny and it is time now for you to arise, go forth and be all of what God called you into this world to be. I pray that the anointing on this book permeates your soul so that you receive the deliverance intended for you at this very moment. May God bless and keep you as you move into the next level of your earthly journey!

—Dr. Roxanna Perry, Pastor of The Shepherd's House of Restoration

Printed in the United States
78114LV00002B/157-189